STAND OUT
from the Crowd
"99 Tips for Successful
& Powerful Presenting"

Michael Trigg

Published by

PRESENTATION SKILLS COACHING

www.presentationskillscoaching.co.uk

First published in Great Britain in 2010 by Presentation Skills Coaching
Tel: 0208 237 5600
info@presentationskillscoaching.co.uk
www.presentationskillscoaching.co.uk

Edited by Marie-Louise Cook of Clever Marketing Systems Ltd.
Design and layout by Clever Marketing Systems Ltd, Waterlooville, Hampshire.
Tel: 023 9226 1212
www.clevermarketingsystems.com

Printed in Great Britain by the
MPG Books Group, Bodmin and King's Lynn

British Library Cataloguing in Publication Data.

ISBN 978-0-9565691-0-3

CONTENTS

INTRODUCTION

Time magazine surveyed its readership some years ago. One of the questions asked was: "What are you biggest fears?" Third from the top of the list came fear of bugs, spiders and creepy crawlies, second was fear of heights and flying - and top of the list by a large margin was fear of standing up and speaking in public. Death apparently rated seventh on this list of things people dreaded most!

Some of you may be reading this because you are keen to raise your game in this vital skill, others will skim it for the odd gem - just to fine tune your existing excellence - you are all welcome.

Our response to making presentations varies hugely. But it would be fair to say that it is very, very rarely top of people's favourite things to do. And many of us go to extraordinary lengths to avoid having to make a presentation.

Why is this so?
For some of you reading this, what I'm about to say will make no sense at all. The remainder will recognise it in varying degrees. The reason is fear. What sort of fear? Fear of failure. Is that all? Fear of failure through ridicule - being made to look stupid, bumbling, being unprofessional, being embarrassed, that our nerves will show, that our voice will crack, the sweat will pour and surely everyone will be judging us in a very critical and negative manner.

You would expect me to be biased but being able to present coherently and naturally and to ENGAGE with any audience is a vital skill. Failing to do so damages promotion prospects in most organisations, loses both existing and potential clients, gives woolly confusing messages, de-motivates staff and in many cases does your self-esteem no favours.

Getting most of it "right" can go a very long way to winning business, getting your ideas accepted, building trust and faith in you and improving other's perceptions of you - both personally and professionally.

Is there one way of doing it - a foolproof magic pill or method? Frankly no. We are each of us unique, with our own personalities and style. And I would ALWAYS encourage you to let your natural style - the real you - come out to play. But it will normally only feel safe to come out and play if you feel you have the tools and the techniques to do justice both to yourself and the subject you are talking about.

That's what this book is about. It is a distillation of the most useful techniques and attitudes that I have been teaching and also learning from my clients for over 20 years. They all work. They work time and time again and in almost every context. Try them for yourself, and experience the difference that even just a few of them can make. It can be the difference that makes the difference.

Do feel free to write to me and share what you have done.

I'd welcome it.

Michael Trigg

SOME FUNDAMENTALS

TIP 1 Let us start this journey together with exploding a modern myth. When you say "presentations" to people, around 90% will immediately think of PowerPoint. How many slides they can produce and how much should go on them. They then spend ages composing those slides, with hardly a thought of how they will talk about them. To them, the slides are the presentation and they are merely the voice accompaniment. This is completely wrong and more importantly, will almost always FAIL TO ENGAGE your audience. So leave any thoughts of PowerPoint behind for now.

TIP 2 Think of a few examples of some really good public speakers and presenters - people who have impressed and engaged you. Now take a sheet of paper and write down the answer to this question: What do they DO? What do they DEMONSTRATE or seem to POSSESS? Do this exercise now before reading any further.

TIP 3 Everything to do with spoken communication essentially falls into two baskets - "what" you say, and "how" you say it. Now, if you review the list of qualities from 2 above - in which basket do most of those comments belong? Most belong in the "how you say it" basket, do they not? This is a very important learning.

TIP4 Less than 10% of the meaning of your communication is carried by your words. Over 90% of the meaning you wish to convey is carried by your voice and how you use it, and by your physiology - how you stand, move and look at people. One of the greatest orators of ancient Greece was Demosthenes. He was once asked for his advice on how to make a speech and his reply was short and to the point: "There are only three things you need to remember: delivery, delivery and delivery." The delivery is the "How."

TIP 5 This is not to imply for one moment that your content is unimportant. It is vital. What it does mean is that you can have the best content in the world but if you can't deliver it in an engaging fashion then it has very little chance of being remembered or acted upon. So you need good content as well as the ability to deliver well.

TIP 6 Any speaker or presenter has three "duties" or obligations to their audience: The first duty is to be interesting. How? By using your voice and physiology to good effect and being engaging. It also helps if you are interested in your subject. But sometimes you won't be. There are times when we have to deliver material that bores or fails to engage us - that's life. In which case be brief. Your lack of interest then has less chance to "leak."

TIP 7 The second duty is to get your message across. How? By being interesting and engaging, and by structuring it well. You also need a message and that's something that many talks simply don't have. Too many are just information dumps. Structure will be covered in more detail later.

TIP 8 The last of these three duties is to let your personality come across - to be you, to be authentic. There is something instinctively engaging about a presenter when they are being themselves. This is most easily achieved when you know your subject, have a clear message and have minimal but powerful and visual notes that support you.

TIP 9 There should not be a mismatch between the person they see presenting and the person they have lunch/coffee/dinner with afterwards. Be natural and authentic; you will more easily build rapport and trust with members of your audience who want to come up and talk to you individually after your presentation.

"My session with Michael has been hugely valuable and I thoroughly recommend working with him. He is incredibly encouraging and knows how to get the best from people. After just one day, Michael completely changed my attitude and approach to presenting and I am now armed with excellent techniques and some new found confidence. I can't thank him enough! "

Jennifer McMahon
Weber Shandwick

THE "HOW" - VOICE

TIP 10 Pitch or intonation. Avoid being monotone at all costs. It is vital that you vary it - slightly more than you would in everyday speech. To do so, keep your volume high, use your arms and hands to gesture and keep your chin at least horizontal. If you lower your chin too often to consult or worse, read your notes, it will have the effect of flattening your pitch to a monotone. If you have a flat tone, not only will you sound boring but you will send your audience into a deeper trance.

TIP 11 Volume. This is a major part of the energy you display. Different venues require different levels of volume. Remember that people's bodies are like sponges for sound, as are curtains, thick carpets and soft furnishings. Imagine that someone at the back of the room is a little deaf in one ear, and you want to reach and engage them. But remember to vary it. Speak loudly for authority and enthusiasm, and also drop your volume for variety and to invite careful listening.

TIP 12 Clarity and enunciation. This is normally solved by speaking loudly enough.

TIP 13 Pace. This is a mixture of speed and ideas per minute. Speed first. Vary it - use it like the accelerator or gearbox of your car. You wouldn't drive for a whole journey in third gear at 3,400rpm.

TIP 14 Pace - ideas per minute. Your central nervous system/unconscious brain is taking in billions of bits of information per second from the cosmos. But your conscious brain - and those of the audience - can only handle 7 +/- 2 bits of information at any one time. Any more than that and it becomes overloaded - however well educated or intelligent you or your audience are. So avoid cramming in too many facts and figures at any one time. To help impart information effectively...

TIP 15 Use word pictures, analogies or metaphors. By doing so, you engage the visual part of the brain. Confucius once said "I hear, I forget. I see, I remember. I do, I understand." So rather than describe an oil field as producing 60,000 barrels a day, maybe experiment with "Imagine the dome of the Capitol building in Washington DC filling up with oil every day. That's what this field produces, and it would be enough to supply the energy needs of the City of London for a month."

TIP 16 Pauses. These are vital. They give you time to breathe, and also give your audience the chance to breathe mentally. Use them like punctuation - a small pause for a comma, bigger pause for a full stop, and an even larger pause between paragraphs. VERY few presenters pause for long enough. When we are nervous or excited, the adrenalin coursing round our bodies distorts our sense of timing. What in reality is a second often feels like eight seconds when in front of an audience. You will rarely pause for long enough.

TIP 17 Signposts. Give good clear signposts between parts of your talk - really clear and obvious ones. For example, "That was the first part of my talk which covered lessons learned from last month; now let me move on to the second part which deals with how we are going to apply them over the next few weeks." PAUSE. "Now, let's take the lessons we learned from our invoicing department..." Avoid being subtle. Make them very obvious and very clear.

TIP 18 Language. As a rule of thumb, use short words, short sentences and "Old words" - words that have been in current usage for over 40 years. One of the biggest and most common mistakes is to alienate your audience by using jargon and too many three-letter abbreviations. Every profession and company has its own jargon. At best, jargon is like a shorthand language between fellow professionals. But it is rarely used at its best. It is mostly used because people are too lazy to think of a plain English, French, Russian or Spanish equivalent, or because they want to exclude others. "If you don't know what I'm talking about then you aren't part of my club." What rubbish. As a working rule, imagine your audience are all aged about 16 years old, fiercely intelligent but with extremely low boredom thresholds. If you can hold an audience of 16 year olds, then you are doing well.

"...Michael first worked with me 15 years ago... helped hone and develop my skills, which I use to this day. Since then, I've taken Michael to 4 different companies... introduced him to senior plc executives who've worked personally with him to develop their skills... all of it a huge success. Everybody who's worked with him has said "That's the best course I've ever been on/the best person I've ever worked with. **"**

Tim Hancock
Group Business Director, Connaught plc

THE "HOW" - PHYSIOLOGY

TIP 19 Generally, you can get away with most things as long as they don't become distracting or irritating. There are few hard and fast rules, but here are a few guidelines...

TIP 20 Stance. It is useful both for comfort and visual authority to stand most of the time with your weight equally balanced between both feet, imagining a thread running gently up the centre of your spine, pulling you upright. This will make you look balanced, comfortable and authoritative. If you put more weight on one foot, after a time it becomes tired and you will shift to the other, which sets up a slow metronome pattern of movement. Also, one of your shoulders will drop as your pelvic girdle will be at an angle, which doesn't look good or balanced. It can give an impression of being a little unsure of your subject.

TIP 21 Moving or walking around. There are few rules, apart from avoiding being irritating or distracting. Generally, if you want to move or walk, make it purposeful and move from A to B, rather than aimlessly wandering around the stage or head of the table. The way we move when presenting is largely out of conscious awareness, so it can be good either to video yourself or ask a friend beforehand to watch for it and give you feedback afterwards.

TIP 22 Hands. These are hugely useful to express yourself and appear natural and sincere. The good news is that they work best when you don't even think about them! Your unconscious brain knows what to do. Allow them to work and express themselves naturally. It's useful to have a comfortable and natural resting place. This is very personal, but what works superbly for most of us is to clasp them gently in front of you at about navel height, with one hand resting gently in the other as if you are about to applaud. They won't stay there for long: your natural expressive powers will take over unconsciously and you will use them without thinking about them.

TIP 23 Avoid clasping them behind your back in military fashion - too stiff and formal and you won't use them much. Also avoid clasping them in front of you at crutch height for the same reasons. You will also look too defensive. Leave that pose to bouncers and doormen.

TIP 24 Also avoid hands in pockets because it traps one of your most powerful means of expression and if you have money in there, you'll most likely play with it. You, of course, will be consciously unaware of this, but your audience will notice everything. The only time it is useful to put your hands in your pockets is when you wish to create a relaxed and collegiate atmosphere and you have established good rapport with your audience. Otherwise, you run the risk of looking casual or disrespectful.

TIP 25 Avoid leaning your hands on the table or clasping the sides of a podium. If you trap or restrict your hands, the natural energy in your body will find another outlet - normally by shifting from foot to foot or swaying or twisting your torso. The energy in your body needs to come out from the hips upwards, not below the hips.

TIP 26 Facial expression. Coco Chanel said "Nobody notices what the best-dressed women are wearing." A strange thing for a couturier to say but maybe what she meant was: if you are appropriately or elegantly dressed and if there are no distractions like a large belly or décolletage, or a tie that looks as if you're wearing it for a bet, then other people's eyes naturally come to rest on the most interesting part of your physiology - namely the top 12 inches - your face. And your face wants to be engaging. We've got 60 sets of muscles in the face, and they might be called "the great unemployed"! Smile frequently and especially at the start - and look as if YOU are engaged. It relaxes and engages the audience.

TIP 27 Eye contact 1: This tip is about involvement and engagement. Absolutely vital. Aim at having eye contact 95% of the time with 100% of the audience. If you want to look at your notes or your laptop - fine. Just pause when you do so. It is "bad manners" to talk to your audience and not look at them.

TIP 28 Eye contact 2: This tip is about the typical traps you can fall into. It is hugely tempting to focus on a friendly face that is smiling and nodding approval or agreement. Avoid giving them too much eye contact - it may feel good and reassuring for you but it will most likely make them very uncomfortable and, more importantly, you will be failing to engage all the others in the room. Also avoid "flitting" (when your eyes dart around the room, never stopping or resting to engage with anybody): it can look shifty and slightly out of control.

TIP 29 Eye contact 3: This tip is about ensuring you engage everyone in a large audience. If you are going to talk, say in an auditorium, it is ALWAYS a good idea to get there early and practise getting on the stage, moving to where you will speak from, and checking in which directions and at which angle you will have to look to engage all of your audience. When you stand up to do the real thing, you will know where to look. This is vital when you are under a spotlight and the audience is in relative darkness. It will feel really strange - talking into the blackness - but your audience will love it. They will feel that you are talking directly to them, and you will be. You just can't see them.

TIP 30 Eye contact 4: This tip is about how to engage people when you are all seated around a table. When you are presenting sitting down to a number of people, the temptation is to look straight ahead of you or at whom you perceive to be the most important person. Mistake. What you are unlikely to know are the true dynamics across that table. One of them may well be tasked with liaising with you and your company. Look at everyone.

TIP 31 Eye contact 5: This tip is about making sure you make eye contact with everybody seated around a table. When you leave the room, the senior person will consult her colleagues and most likely ask their opinion. If you haven't looked at them, because you've been focussing on the senior person, then you won't have engaged them and their reactions will be at best indifferent or most likely negative. That alone could lose you the business.

THE "WHAT" - STRUCTURE

The Introduction

TIP 32 A good talk needs a shape. Otherwise it can become just a rambling information dump. And if we borrow a thought from ancient Chinese Traditional Medicine and the Indian Ayurveda - both 5,000 years old - prevention is better than cure.

TIP 33 If you start well and engage their brains and interest, and "lay out your stall" clearly, then what follows becomes so much easier.

TIP 34 Benjamin Franklin said "If you seek to persuade, appeal to the interest rather than the intellect." With what follows, we shall seek to do both.

The Funnel

TIP 35 One of the best ways to start any talk is with a funnel. Imagine the shape of a funnel - Y shaped - very wide at the top and with a small aperture at the bottom, which leads into the subject or topic of your talk. You start with a statement that everyone can recognise or agree with - it starts to get their attention - and then you narrow the content of your funnel more and more until you get to its essence, namely your subject or topic. This is a superb and professional way to build rapport and seize audience attention.

TIP 36 Example1. Suppose the topic is Global Warming. Here is a possible funnel: "Good morning. From time to time, most nations are faced with huge challenges, be it warfare, revolution, drought or dealing with a credit crunch. But it is very rare for the whole of humanity to be faced with the same challenge at the same time. We, all of us, are faced with just such a challenge - and the clock is ticking - which brings me to my subject today: Global Warming and what we individually can do about it."

TIP 37   Example 2. Suppose the topic is Coca Cola. A possible funnel might be "Good afternoon, ladies and gentlemen. Almost every company dreams of having a brand which is instantly recognisable, universally popular and the market leader in its sector. I want to talk about such a brand today, how it achieved its dominance, how it has maintained it for decades, and the lessons we can learn from its success and its mistakes - and that brand is Coca Cola."

TIP 38   Example 3. Suppose the topic is your Monthly Report/Update To Your Team. A possible funnel could be "'Morning everyone. As we know it's been a challenging few months. I don't know about you, but I can't remember when we last faced so many changes both with our customers and the economy, so let's take stock of how well we've done... the Monthly Update."

TIP 39   Example 4. Suppose the topic/context is your presentation of your product/service to a potential client. "Good morning Mrs/Mr X. We both know that both of us face ever increasing competition and the need to deliver top quality and utterly reliable service is no longer an option - it's the only way to stay in business. I believe we have a track record to be proud of in these areas, and I'd like to show you how we, Phoenix International, might be of service and value to you."

TIP 40 Notice how all the examples are quite brief. You can take up to 15-20 seconds, but I recommend keeping it fairly brief, particularly with cultures that are quite direct - Central European, Russian, Dutch, Flemish and some Scandinavians, for example.

TIP 41 After you have stated your topic - the subject of your talk - have the courage to pause. Let it hang in the air, so that your audience are in no doubt as to what you are talking about. Too many of us just gabble straight on, and unless members of the audience are listening intently, it is quite likely they will miss what the talk is about. So pause.

TIP 42 Now is the time to introduce yourself - not earlier. The majority of presenters start off with their name. This isn't wrong or bad, it's just a little boring. And if you are honest with yourself, it isn't YOU that they've come to listen to... it's what you've come to SAY. So that is why in most cases I would suggest that your topic gets a higher billing than who you are. A useful phrase is "For those of you I haven't met yet..." For example, I say, "For those of you I haven't met yet... I'm Michael Trigg, Director of Phoenix International, and I have been working in personal development full time for X years, and before that I worked for Procter and Gamble, where training and developing others was part of my role as a sales manager and account handler." That's about the longest sentence you'll need. Less is more.

The Aim

TIP 43 Now you come to THE most important part of the whole talk, which I observe is missing in about 90% of presentations. It's the AIM. The purpose of the talk. It states what is in it for them. It gives them a reason for listening to you. There is always only one aim. It is concise and tight and clear. And it is expressed thus: "The AIM of this talk is to... so that..."

TIP 44 Your Compass. Sometimes the AIM will be really obvious to you, and at other times you may take hours to decide what it is, then hone it to a tight, concise statement. It is the beacon, the guiding light, the compass that will guide and dictate the direction and content of your talk. It is well worth investing a little time in getting this right. It can save you hours of fruitless and irrelevant preparation and it will help you keep all your content relevant and focussed.

TIP 45 Focus. Not only will it do that for your content, it will keep your audience focussed too.

TIP 46 Can't find an AIM? If you happen to struggle with the question "Just what IS my AIM?" then think along these lines: think what you want your audience to do or think differently as a result of listening to you. That should give you the answer.

TIP 47 Put yourself in their shoes. Another very powerful way of finding out what your audience want to hear and to decide and refine your aim is to put yourself in their shoes. The Sioux Indians had a saying "Great Spirit. Teach me not to judge another man until I have walked six weeks in his moccasins." One way of doing this very effectively is to use different perceptual positions. To do this you need plenty of space - like a training room or a board room or similar. Anywhere will do, as long as you have room - even outdoors. But keeping it indoors makes it more realistic.

TIP 48 You don't need to know them personally. However, this works most powerfully if you do know and have met the people who will be in your audience. But even if you haven't met them, you can still get real value from this process. Start with a particular individual in mind and then sit in one of the audience chairs. Pretend to be him. Sit as he would sit, adopt his body language as far as possible. Then imagine taking on his thinking - his goals, aspirations, worries, fears, etc. Of course, it is make-believe - you will never know exactly what he is thinking - but it is a very informed make-believe. Then ask yourself, still pretending to be this audience member "What do I want to get from this presentation? What do I want the speaker to address or cover?" Write down what you discover.

TIP 49 Then get up and move to a different chair and start the process again. Sit as they would sit, take on their thinking as far as you can, and ask again "What do I want from this? What will make this a worthwhile use of my time?" If you get into the role, and "play" with intent, you will surprise yourself with what you learn about what your audience want. Even if you have never met them, you can still imagine how a director, contract manager, designer or supervisor might sit and how they might think.

TIP 50 The Power of Perceptual Positions. What you've just read may sound a little fanciful and far-fetched, but it can be truly powerful. It can give you an insight into the minds of the audience that is effective and quick. It takes about 20 minutes to go through this, and you'll get faster with experience. I have taught this for many years to my clients and without exception they found it at worst valuable and at best revelatory. In a different but still relevant context, I once coached someone in preparation for an internal interview panel. The panel was made up of six people: four of whom he knew well, and the remaining two just by sight. My client was being interviewed for promotion to partner in one of the world's largest property consultancies. It took us about 30 minutes to go through all perceptual positions of the interview panel. In this case we were not looking for material to refine his Aim. We were seeking to discover what questions he might be asked. I think we came up with a list of 20 or so major if not killer questions, after sitting as each panel member would sit, taking on their mindset, and then imagining what questions they might ask. He told me later that during the interview he had been asked every single one of those questions verbatim. It's a powerful technique. Check it out.

TIP 51 Some examples of AIMs, using Tips 36, 37, 38, and 39 above. 36: Topic - Global Warming: "The aim of this talk about Global Warming is to highlight some the things you and I can do individually, so that should you choose, you can reduce your personal carbon footprint."

TIP 52 Example of an AIM for Tip 37: Topic - Coca Cola: "The purpose of the next 20 minutes is to look at some of the advertising and marketing that Coca Cola has done over the last 30 years, so that you can apply some of their successes to your own brands and also avoid some of their more costly mistakes."

TIP 53 Example of an AIM for Tip 38: Topic - Monthly Report/Update: "The aim of this talk is to give you an update of where we are against our objectives so that you have a clearer idea of what is working well and what still needs to be addressed."

TIP 54 Example of an AIM for Tip 39: Topic - Your Product/Service: "The aim of this presentation is to give you a flavour of who we are, our track record, what we do and how we do it, so that you are better able to decide if we're the sort of people you'd like to work with."

The Agenda

TIP 55 Now it is time to set out your stall: your Agenda.

TIP 56 It is best to keep the number of Agenda items to three. Why? Because your audience are most unlikely to take away any more than three. You can say a lot within three items. If you really need more, then make it five not four. The brain retains odd numbers better than even.

TIP 57 Example. "I want to cover this in three parts. Firstly, we will look at the scientific research behind global warming. Secondly, we'll look at the effects and how and why time is running out for us all and thirdly, we'll cover some practical things that you and your family can do to make a difference."

TIP 58 Recap: Tips 32 to 54 cover your introduction. Look at what you've achieved. You have hooked your audience in with the funnel. They know what you are going to talk about - the subject. They know who you are and why you're qualified to talk to them, and they know what's in it for them as a result of listening to you - the AIM. And they know the scope of what you are going to cover - all within the first 30 seconds to a minute. You have covered all the main areas your audience will be thinking about, whether consciously or unconsciously.

The Main Body

TIP 59 That is the most important part dealt with. Now let us make sure that the three items on your main body are clear and easy to follow. This is principally down to clear signposting.

TIP 60 Signposting is done by giving really clear verbal pointers - backwards whence you came, and forwards to where you are going. "That covers my first section, which was all about the How - namely delivery. Now let me move on to the second part, which is all about structure." Then pause so there is a clear gap, a silence, between the two sections. Avoid the temptation to be subtle here. If you make too subtle a transition between sections, then unless your audience is hanging on every word, they are likely to miss it. They will then quickly become disoriented and wonder where they are in your talk, or indeed where you are. Be really blatant and obvious - this is not a time for subtlety. "That was my second point about Y. Now let's move on to my third and final part, which is about Z."

The Summary

TIP 61 Tell them what you told them. The Introduction was telling them what you were about to tell them. The Main Body was telling them. And in the Summary, you are going to tell them what you told them. You hear this format every day on the news: the news headlines then the news stories behind the headlines then finally the headlines again.

TIP 62 First of all, flag to the audience that you are entering the summary. "In summary/in conclusion/wrapping this up" etc. Use some form of sentence that lets them know what you're doing.

TIP 63 Then recap the Agenda. For example, "We covered three main points today. Firstly, we covered the research behind Global Warming. Secondly, we looked at the effects and how and why time is running out for us all and thirdly, we looked at some practical things that you and your family can do to make a difference."

TIP 64 Use the same language in the summary that you used in setting out the Agenda. This is because your audience want a feeling of coming home, of familiarity, of rounding things off. If you use different words or terms, you might sow confusion in their minds. They might start to question and wonder if you did indeed cover those points, and most adults do not like being confused. It will lessen the power of your talk and the thrust of your message if you change the wording in the summary agenda.

TIP 65 Now return to your Aim and restate it - they will most likely have forgotten what it was, and as this is the most important message in your whole talk, it bears repetition. e.g. "The Aim of this talk this morning was to highlight some of the things that you and I can do individually about global warming, so that if you choose to, you can reduce your personal carbon footprint."

TIP 66 If there is any action or next step you'd like them to take, this is the time to state or ask it - after you have restated the Aim.

TIP 67 Finally, to finish off with a flourish, you can funnel out. It is the opposite of funnelling in. At the start of your talk, you funnelled from the general down to the specific of your subject. At the end, should you choose, you can go from the specific to the general. For example, "I hope that I've given you some food for thought and even more importantly some suggestions for action. Individually we are like tiny pixels on a screen. Add all the millions of pixels together and we get a full picture. Will you be part of that picture? Because what we do now will determine if we can look our children and future grandchildren in the face. Thank you."

VISUAL AIDS & SLIDES

TIP 68 Last, not first. I started in Tip 1 with a sincere but rather abrasive note about slides. Used well, they can be a fantastic tool, and a horrid and boring irrelevance if not. If nothing else, please follow this principle. Get the Aim, structure and content of your presentation together first. Then and only then create the slides to back it up.

TIP 69 Software. Most people and certainly most corporates are PC people, and a small but growing percentage are Mac people. Microsoft's presentation tool is PowerPoint, and Apple's is Keynote. They are both excellent, but Keynote allows you to create much more interesting transitions and builds and it is very easy to master. These hold the audience's attention and interest more. If it's important for you to show slides and you give a lot of slide presentations and create them yourself then do check out a Macbook and use it for your presentations. It's worth the investment. Any Apple store will demonstrate Keynote to you, and then you can make your own decision. MacBooks aren't cheap but are well built and have come down in price, and the software is surprisingly inexpensive.

TIP 70 As a rule of thumb, have a slide for the Aim, and one for the Agenda. Have duplicates that you can come back to in your summary.

TIP 71 Another rule of thumb - the content should fit onto the front of a T shirt. Less is more.

TIP 72 Avoid reading them! There are exceptions to every rule. That said, think long and hard before reading off a slide. The audience will accept you reading a few but will become bored or irritated very quickly.

TIP 73 With bullet points, use them as headlines to talk around. This keeps their minds busy, as they listen for links between the few words in the slide and how you are building and talking about them.

TIP 74 If you really need to have a lot of bullet points on a slide, then build them cleverly. Reveal one, then three, then one, then two etc. They never know quite what is coming. Helps keep them alert.

TIP 75 Where appropriate use images, pictures, photographs with a few words. Far more memorable.

TIP 76 Handing out copies beforehand. Too often I see exact copies of the slides being handed out before the presentation. This is useful during a training session or long seminar, as delegates and students are making notes on and beside them and they are usually part of a hefty file of material. Yet they are often given out for no real reason, custom usually. I would suggest handing them nicely prepared and personalised blank booklets or pads on which to make their notes. Tell them that they will be getting a copy of all your slides immediately after your talk. Some may protest, but at least they will be concentrating on your talk and the slides you are showing. Otherwise they will be flicking through their copies of the slides to find something more interesting or searching for the slide you are currently talking about. And woe betide you if you have amended the slide you are showing but not the slide pack. It's happened to most of us at some time, both as speaker and audience!

TIP 77 A simple but important final point about any visual aid. Make sure the audience can see it/ them. It's a surprising but salient thought that most presentation suites are usually designed by people who never have to use them. There is nearly always a central screen filling much of the wall and a podium to the side where the speaker is expected to remain, like a prisoner in the dock. If at all feasible, step away from the podium so that you can move your hands and arms and also the audience can see all of you. You will also be less tempted to grip onto the sides of the podium. Ensure that when you find a new and better position to stand, you do not stand in the way of the slides. If in doubt, ask your audience if they can see.

"Michael is a very dedicated and passionate teacher with great influencing and motivating skills. Very proficient and very thorough. With a great sense of humour that brings knowledge across in such an highly entertaining way, makes you almost feel guilty how much fun it is. Highly recommended. "

Lutz Stoever,
International Marketing Manager,
Universal Music Group International

PREPARATION & NOTE-MAKING

TIP 78 First, decide your Aim. Write it in full. For example, "The Aim of this presentation is... so that you can..." One of the best ways to gather your thoughts for a talk is to brainstorm. Start with a plain unlined sheet of A4 paper. Put the title of your talk in the centre, preferably with a small image or symbol that represents it then let your thoughts cascade in random fashion. Start with a line radiating a couple of inches outwards from the central image, then add your thought as a single word at the end of that line. Then draw a line from that word/thought and add another word/thought. And continue word - line - word - line. When you run out of space or that theme is expended, go back to the middle and start with a new line then a new thought then a new line, etc, etc.

TIP 79 Some of the ideas which cascade from the richness of your thoughts and memories will seem utterly nonsensical and irrelevant. No matter. Keep going. They are by-products of the creative process. Keep this up for about 5-10 minutes maximum. Your piece of paper will most likely be covered in a mess of lines and words - perfect! You have been allowing the right side of your brain a bit of free rein. This is the part of your brain responsible for memory, pictures, conceptual thinking, intuition and spatial awareness, amongst others.

TIP 80 Next, clarify your Aim. Look at what you wrote in Tip 78. Is it still the same? Can you tighten or improve it? Do you need to change it completely? Or is it perfect as it is?

TIP 81 Decide your three Agenda headings, which will support the Aim. Write them down. Then, take a pack of highlighters (Stabilo seem the best) and highlight each Agenda item in a different colour.

TIP 82 Now we retreat to more familiar territory and also the left side of the brain, responsible for logic, analysis, calculation, language, sequential thinking and memorising. No surprise that it is sometimes called the "adult" or "academic" side of the brain. We are going to select what is relevant, and reject what isn't. There are three criteria for this. A) Does it help with the Aim. If not, reject it. B) How long are you speaking for? 5, 10, 20 or 30 minutes? Select the content to fit the time. C) The Audience.

TIP 83 What do you want to know about your audience?

- Level of knowledge of your subject
- Previous experience of what you're suggesting
- Their expectations
- Level of interest
- Time of day you'll be speaking. People are normally more receptive and sharper in the morning. If you are speaking mid to late afternoon, make it high on energy and low on detail
- Any prejudice
- Culture.

TIP 84 Different countries and cultures. If you do business with other nationalities, get a copy of "When Cultures Collide" by Richard Lewis. It's one of the best and most readable books available on this tricky but important subject. One of my clients has over 60 different nationalities working for them. For several years, I have taken this book to my trainings there, and encouraged my delegates to look up the chapter on their own country and check it for accuracy. Over 80% say that it is uncannily accurate.

TIP 85 Now take one of the three highlighters that you've used to colour your Agenda items. Go over your brainstorm and highlight everything you wish to include under that Agenda point. Then pick up the second highlighter and do likewise. Then the third. Anything that has not been highlighted or selected will not be used.

TIP 86 Finally, create your notes. There are many, many ways of doing this, but I find a variation on mind mapping the most effective. There are many excellent books on mind mapping; some of the best are by Tony Buzan. I teach a variation of mind mapping that is more effective for presentations. They look like amoebas gathered around a central image - your topic. It is something best seen demonstrated, and frankly I will more likely confuse rather than help you by attempting to do it justice here. I cover this is in detail on my distance learning product, The Complete Presenter. You'll soon be able to buy it online from my website. It's in the form of an iPod touch, with explanatory slides and a video demonstration of how to create these amoeba notes, and much, much more. As far as I can tell, there is nothing like it on the market.

TIP 87 The notes I show you how to create are quite simply the most effective tool on the planet for effective, natural, engaging presenting. No one has ever shown me anything more powerful. They allow you to talk "as if" not using notes and to sound and look natural and spontaneous. You will have eye contact 95% of the time with your audience, you will never lose your way, and you can take questions and interruptions at any stage and still find you way back on track.

You won't miss anything out and you'll look and sound confident and professional and human. Sound magic? It is! These notes will lift you to a new level of fluency, competence and confidence, which is my guarantee to you when you've bought and used The Complete Presenter or after you've worked with me personally. Oh, and they can cut the time it takes to prepare by up to 90%.

TIP 88 In the meantime, here are some tips for making useful notes with what you have. Firstly, write very little. Use keywords that you can talk from and around.

TIP 89 Wherever possible, use pictures and symbols rather than words. You may not think you can draw, and of course some of us are more adept than others! But even a spidery symbol or wonky logo will beat words 19 times out of 20. Over nearly 25 years, I have trained literally thousands of people aged from 13 to 75 from almost every nationality around the world and in almost every sector. Despite initial suspicion and sometimes incredulity, I can count on the fingers of two hands those that have preferred afterwards to stick only with words rather than a mixture of words and pictures. The universal saying "A picture's worth a thousand words" could have been coined for presentation notes.

TIP 90 Use plenty of colour but in a disciplined way. Create a colour code. Have a separate colour for each Agenda item, one for the Aim, another for visual aids, so that you know when to show them. Have fun experimenting.

TIP 91 Use space and shape. Avoid bunching all your ideas tightly together: give them space to breathe on the page, and surround each section (Introduction, Main Body 1, 2, 3, Summary) with their own shape. Trace a solid flowing continuous line around what you have written and drawn for each section - this will create a unique amoeba-like shape, which is easily memorable to the brain. Then apply the relevant highlighter to this amoeba line/boundary. Now each section will have its own shape and colour. The brain loves this. Just try it. Experiment. Even if you ignore most of this and just use colours, key words and symbols and pictures, you will be so far ahead of the game.

" I have always disliked giving presentations and wanted to know how people do this successfully without sounding like they are reading from a script. Michael gave me the tools to do this and the confidence to go on to speak in front of 150 people. His patience, understanding and obvious skills make this a painless and dare I say enjoyable process! **"**

Penny Verbe,
CEO of Smoke & Mirrors

HANDLING QUESTIONS

TIP 92 This is an area that gives many of us cause for concern. Particularly unexpected questions when you're in the middle of your flow. I know, because it is high on the list of objectives of those I work with. Much of the sting can be taken out of this by clear positioning. Let your audience know up front how you suggest handling questions; in effect, you are laying down the rules whilst inviting them to agree to them. It works in 95 cases out of 100. A good place to do this is right at the end of the introduction. And there are three principle methods: The first is where you can offer to take questions at any time. This is very open and transparent and works best when you know your subject well, you don't have a time limit, and there are no more than 10 people in the audience. If these conditions don't apply, then opt for the second method: say that you'd be delighted to take questions and to that end you will be pausing after each agenda item to take questions then. Ask them if they'd be good enough to keep their questions for those slots. This allows you time to get a fair amount of your message across, before you stop for interaction. It makes for a nice balance between content and interaction. Safest of all is the third method: say that you welcome questions, and that you will be leaving time for them at the end. Then when you get to the end, take your questions BEFORE and not after the summary. About 90% of presenters open it up for questions after they have summarised. Then after 5 or 10 minutes of questions and discussion, what will their audience remember of their carefully crafted presentation? The answers to the last few questions or maybe even just the answer to the last one! All that effort for naught.

TIP 93 To lie or not to lie? I wouldn't. It has taken years to build your reputation, and you can destroy it in a few seconds with an untruth. Of course, you can be artfully vague, or give a parallel example. For example, "Well, I haven't got the figures for Italy, but I do have some for Spain, which has a very similar consumption pattern." That's not lying. However, if you really don't know the answer, admit it. Be honest. You cannot know everything. There will always be a question that from time to time gets under your armour. That's life. So rather than view it as a failure on your part or that you're somehow being unprofessional (you could do, but why would you?) see it rather as an opportunity to get in front of them again and shine. Make a note of the question. The simple act of writing it down shows them you are taking it seriously. Then under-promise and over-deliver. If you agree to get back to them by Thursday, bust a gut to get back with an answer by Tuesday. Imagine how impressed you'd be with such a response.

TIP 94 Here is a little acronym and technique for handling questions well and professionally. It's called TRACT, and it's designed to do several things... make the questioner feel appreciated, stop you leaping down their throat with the answer, give you time to think, and keep everybody involved...

TIP 95 The T stands for Thank. "Thank you Michael for that question."

TIP 96 R stands for Repeat or Rephrase. The first is often necessary in a largish group. Someone near the front may ask you a question that people at the back of the room cannot hear. "I don't know if you all heard what Michael asked me, but what he wanted to know was..."

Or a Rephrase: "So Michael, let me just clarify what I think you are asking me. What I believe you are asking is... Is that correct?"

TIP 97 A is for Answer. Beware the trap here. All our instincts teach us to engage and look at the person who has asked us the question. It's part of our education and considered "good manners". And if you do so, the questioner will be very pleased as she will feel you are engaging directly with her. But you will have lost most of the rest of the audience, who may have no interest in her question or your answer to it. Now you are not even looking at them. Perfect excuse to talk to the person next to them or check their Blackberry. Either way you've lost them. So, when answering a question, answer it to the WHOLE audience. This will keep everyone, questioner and audience involved.

TIP 98 C is for Check back. "Have I covered that to your satisfaction?" If yes, everyone's happy. If not, then you get another bite at the cherry.

TIP 99 T is for Thank them again. "Thanks for that question Michael." Try TRACT out. It sounds and is remarkably effective.

"...as a result of the fantastic work he did, he has since been referred across the organisation and the group. He has been a delight to work with... real passion and commitment and many years of experience... I have no hesitation whatsoever in recommending him. Michael cares about what he does and delivers value each and every time. **"**

Connie Phillips,
Head of Learning and Development,
CMG Europe

CONCLUSION

I hope that you've found this small book useful. None of what I've said here is revolutionary, and that is the way it should be. And it all works. Time after time I have been privileged enough to have been the catalyst in helping my clients transform the way they engage both with audiences and with themselves.

All of us are unique and have our own style and way of being. And if you look back over these 99 tips, you will find nothing that requires you to be other than yourself. Yet when you apply them, more of you seems to become available to your audience - and as audiences - and human beings - we respond well to that on many levels.

We all spend most of our waking lives in some form of communication. It's probably the most crucial skill in life. We all have a fundamental need to be understood and to understand others. By presenting clearly, confidently, engagingly and honestly, you will be building your reputation and that of your organisation.

You will create clarity and confidence where it might have been absent, and you will be serving your clients and your colleagues by taking the trouble to do this well. I wish you well and if you are moved to let me know the difference these Tips make to you, then please mail me at michael@presentationskillscoaching.co.uk. I will be genuinely delighted to hear from you.

Dame Edith Evans' advice to the young actress Joan Plowright:

"My dear, when you get up on that stage, some people will not like your chemistry. If they don't like your chemistry, at least let them admire your skill."

READ WHAT OTHERS SAY...

"...I learned something new about the presentation of myself and my ideas, and it made me more effective. The second pleasant surprise is the effect the training has had on us as an organisation. We've become collectively a lot clearer in what we have to say, we've become a lot more self-confident, open and accessible... and I think part of the credit is due to Michael Trigg and his training. Thoroughly recommended."
Dan Smith, Secretary General of International Alert

"Michael provides a framework that when used for presentations, increases their effectiveness, and thus the effectiveness of the presenter. Building on this presentation architecture, he transformed my personal presentation style using a combination of tools and experience. This combination of new presentation structure and personal style transformed my approach and dramatically improved my effectiveness."
Senior executive, Financial Services Company

"...after the event I had a lot of managers approaching me... wanting Michael to come back and work with their teams and with individuals. Fantastic feedback... very professional... very thorough... I'd recommend Michael thoroughly. From a commercial point of view, you see a true value from the investment."
Anita Way, Director,
Head of Education & Development,
Major Investment Bank

"This man is excellent and I would highly recommend him."
Head of Communications, International Alert

"I got onto Michael's Presentation Skills course 2 years ago, and I must say it's been phenomenal since then. It has improved my confidence, the approach is very simple, and it is something you can just get on and go with. It is amazing. I've recommended to friends that they attend the training, and I have seen the improvement in them. I would highly recommend it any day. And I would suggest that if you do get the opportunity – this is simple. It is no fuzz, it is direct, it is usable... I recommend you get on to it."
Charles Kofi Fekpe, Senior Finance Officer, International Alert

"I found this training to be so useful, and only wish that I had the opportunity to do it earlier! Everything that we learned will be applicable to my work, and I really feel that I learned a huge amount and progressed a long way even though it was only a one-day training. It was so useful that I was happy to sit there for 10 hours!"
Senior Manager, International Alert

"I attended Michael's 2 day course a couple of years ago. Before it, I had a "little bit of an issue" with the whole confidence thing, and a MASSIVE fear that I would forget what I was talking about and completely freeze up. Michael's course helped me massively. Not only have I become a MUCH better presenter, I've also transferred these skills in other areas, particularly with clients. I now talk with much more gravitas, they are compelled and engaged in what I am talking about because I now know how to communicate a lot more efficiently. Thank you Michael, it's been great."
Claire Koryczan, Senior account Manager, FutureBrand

"Just wanted to send an email thanking you on your great course last week. Big 10 out of 10 from me."
Ethan Galloway, Marketing, Universal Music

"I worked with Michael about a year and a half ago. Having worked in the industry for a while and been presenting to clients for many years, I thought "How much more can I learn?" I got a bit cocky about it. But actually, the course was fantastic. It teaches you how to really structure your thoughts, to really read your audience's mind before you walk in so that you can speak and structure your thoughts around them. It teaches you clarity and the pitfalls around what to do and what not to do.

"The benefits for me were realised very soon after the course. We had to go to Egypt to pitch for a job. I remember getting the brief from my boss and thinking 'You can't be serious! 24 hours to turn this job round?' I was beside myself with anxiety, but I really applied the stuff I'd learned from Michael. And in 24 hours I turned it around and created a great presentation with great ideas. Went to Cairo, pitched, and a couple of weeks later we'd learned we'd got the job. And as far as I'm concerned, that wouldn't have been possible without the training course that I attended with Michael."

Nader Khosrovani
Associate Director for Strategy, Futurebrand

"The training course with Michael 14 months ago was absolutely fantastic, and I'd highly recommend it. The course was extremely beneficial not only in terms of presentation skills, but also in my own personal development. It gave me more confidence, which then had a knock on effect when I was handing clients and when I was dealing with people internally. This has led to the possibility of promotion, and makes me feel happier about my everyday work."

Katie Rothschild, Account Manager, Futurebrand

"...I thought there wasn't much I could learn about Presentation Skills, but Michael proved very quickly that you certainly can teach an old dog new tricks... I finished the course thinking it was one of the best I'd ever attended in the whole of my career. As a result, I sent many of my staff to work with him. In this present economic climate, the ability to get your message across to customers both old and new is extremely important. I believe that Michael is one of the best in the industry and I can't recommend him highly enough... if you trust your training to him, you'll be delighted with the results and see the benefits in improved sales and improved skills of your staff."
Tony Hampson, Director, MOR Facilities Management

"...the great thing has been that I now find that I am approaching presentations in a far more confident and relaxed manner... we've been able to secure a considerable amount of work and get our ideas across clearly to our potential customers – and this is due in no small part to the training Michael has given to us. I couldn't recommend his training too strongly."
Allan Broad, Business Development Manager, Connaught plc

"...I've just spent 2 days with Michael 1:1... an excellent experience... I've really exceeded my expectations... feel much more comfortable in engaging with an audience... very convinced that I've made significant progress."
Ralph Odermatt, MD, Group Accounting Policy, UBS AG, Zurich

THE 'COMPLETE PRESENTER' ON AN IPOD TOUCH

Are you on the move a lot? Do you find it hard just to fit all you want into a day, let alone take time out for training or being coached? Or maybe you're looking for an easy and cost-effective way of refining, revising or developing your ability to engage with any client or size of audience.

The Complete Presenter lives up to it's name. Many distance learning programmes are packaged on CDs or DVDs, but this one is preloaded onto an iPod Touch. **It's been designed to be comprehensive, easy and fun to use, and for you to learn at your own pace, where and when you want, and at an affordable price.**

It contains much of what I have taught and also learned from my clients over the last 25 years. **I haven't taken recordings from a live event, but created them especially for this programme.**

When you think back to the number of talks and presentations you've sat through, some will have been outstanding and some painful to endure.

You want to avoid appearing in the second category!

It isn't complicated or difficult to avoid. **When you follow and apply even just some of the learnings in this programme, you can transform your ability to engage with any audience.**

What it contains

The Complete Presenter contains the essence of what I would teach in a 2 day programme, distilled for teaching you 1:1. **You will have hours of proven, pragmatic, transformational content based on over 25 years of practise, experience and success.**

It will address:

- Where you are now.

- The 3 "Duties" of any speaker

- What good speakers do and what we can learn from them

- Your voice, and how to use it to best effect

- Your body language

- How and where to look

- Structure - giving your talk shape

- How to begin any talk powerfully and effectively

- Engaging & building rapport with any audience in 20 seconds - and how to keep it throughout

- Creating and honing your message - and how to get it across

- Ending well - ensure your message is received and understood

- How to cut the time it takes to prepare by up to 90%

- How to create some of the most powerful presenting notes on the planet

- The Art of Persuasion

- How to Influence with Integrity

- 5 Logical Levels - being congruent

- Tips on presenting to different cultures and nationalities

- Handling questions professionally and elegantly

The Complete Presenter is organised into chapters for **easy access and reference and revision.**

You will have access to a **full back up of the material**, downloadable from my site, so if you wipe the content from your iPod Touch, you can replace it easily.

But that's not all!

You get 3 Bonuses when you buy 'The Complete Presenter'

BONUS 1: The Complete Presenter also includes something that is only addressed in the VIP Programme - an interview with Michael Brown, one of the UK's top media trainers. You'll learn some tips and advice he gives when coaching his clients to deal with press and TV. His normal fees are £2,000 a day, and you are getting his advice and experience as part of The Complete Presenter!

BONUS 2: An interview with Sarah Setterfield, a highly experienced image and impression consultant. She will share some powerful advice on making the most of your dress, colouring and physical presence.

BONUS 3: To encourage you to take your learning to the next stage, **we give you £300 off your first 1:1 presentation coaching session.**

Guarantee:

We think you'll be delighted with The Complete Presenter. The Apple iPod Touch is a delight. Slim, light, state of the art, intuitive and easy to use; and the content and slides are unique to this programme. However, if you are not 100% satisfied then return it to us within 30 days and we will give you a complete refund.

To order **The 'Complete Presenter'**, go to
www.presentationskillscoaching.co.uk
or call **0208 237 5600**

1:1 EXECUTIVE PRESENTATION COACHING

It is important for senior management to be able to present and engage well with both existing and potential clients at any time. The current turmoil in the commercial world makes this ever more vital. Being able to establish a rapport with an audience quickly, talk their language and engage with them in a human yet professional way becomes a key skill and even an art.

Every business presentation is an excellent opportunity to differentiate yourself from the competition – both internal as well as external. Equipping clients to do this easily and effectively is my speciality.

To give you encouragement, I have been coaching senior executives in presenting techniques for over 20 years. And like you I have found that rank and seniority are no guarantees of either competence or confidence when presenting.

Goals

I will learn these from you before we start working together, and each programme is tailored and bespoke to your needs. I intuit that they might include confidence building, body language and non verbal communication, greater self awareness,the ability to present fluently and engage with any size or mix of audience; capture and hold attention throughout, cut preparation time, and leave the audience looking forward to the next time you present.

Method

We will work together over 4 sessions of up to 4 hours each. It will be intense yet invigorating, enjoyable and highly productive and effective. I use a combination of utterly pragmatic, proven,highly effective tools and techniques as well as some of the latest and most "cutting edge" brain research and applications.

Each presentation is videoed on HD digital equipment, both for playback and as evidence of progress and growth. You'll receive either a DVD of each session, or an Ipod Touch onto which you can download your videos from my site.

You are treated as an individual and encouraged to make the most of your own unique style and personality without having any "formula" thrust upon you. Yet you will see,hear and feel the difference in the way you present and engage with any group.

Included with the 4 sessions are:

- An iPod Touch

- DVDs

- Personalised, initialed hard back journal.

- Telephone "helpline" coaching for 6 months

Guarantee

Your confidence and skill will at the very least double when you work with me. Absolutely guaranteed. Or it won't cost you a penny.

Benefits of 1:1 Presentation Coaching

- Differentiate and stand out from your competition

- Totally focussed on your needs and outcomes

- Your coaching fits around your schedule and your choice of location

- Total privacy & confidentiality

- Increased fluency, competence, eloquence and professionalism

- Greater self awareness

- Enhanced reputation – have audiences talk about you in increasingly positive terms

- Transformed ability to present to any audience

- Exceed your expectations – both of me and you

- Vastly reduced preparation time

- Engage audiences in a whole new way

- Get your message across every time

- Greater confidence, eloquence and presence

- Win & retain more business

- Gives you the edge – greater chance of promotion

To find out more about our
1:1 Presentation Coaching, email us at
info@presentationskillscoaching.co.uk
or call **0208 237 5600**

PRESENTATION & PERSONAL IMPACT FOR GROUPS

(2 days)

The internet and world wide web have transformed the way we work and even live. It has never been so easy to acquire, send and receive information. And many choose to inform, persuade and influence almost solely via the net. Much of your internal and external competition do this.

So when you have the chance to engage and influence face to face, you will want to make an excellent, coherent, professional and natural impression. Competition has always been a factor and the current turmoil in the commercial world makes this ever more vital. **Why should a colleague or client listen to you or buy what you are suggesting? Spend 2 days with me and you will have the answers. Guaranteed.**

Being able to establish a rapport with an audience quickly, talk their language and engage with them in a human yet professional way becomes a key skill and even an art.

Every business presentation is an opportunity to make a positive impact and be remembered. A chance for you to impress, stand out – and differentiate yourself from the competition – both internal as well as external. Equipping small groups to do this easily and effectively is one of my specialties.

Goals

I will learn these from you at the start of the programme. The content of the 2 days is then dictated by the group's goals.

I intuit that they may include confidence building, body language and non verbal communication, reducing the fear of public speaking,the ability to present fluently and engage with any size or mix of audience,reduce nerves, have an infallible structure, capture and hold attention throughout, cut preparation time, and leave the audience looking forward to the next time you present.

Method

You will give 3 talks over the 2 days, all of them filmed - for playback and as evidence of your progress and growth. Each participant will receive their own DVD , as well as a personalised hard back A4 journal.

All four of you will be encouraged to make the most of your own unique style and personality without having any "formula" thrust upon you. Yet there will be a recognisable consistency in the greatly improved way you present and engage with any group.

Included in the training:

- DVDs

- Hard backed A4 personalised journals

- Telephone help line coaching for 6 months

Guarantee

Your confidence and skill will at the very least double when you work with me. Absolutely guaranteed. Or it won't cost you a penny.

Benefits of Presentation & Personal Impact Training in a Small Group

- Learn from each other as well as the tutor

- Practise and learn in a small group dynamic – challenging yet safe

- More economical than 1:1 coaching

- Increased fluency, competence, eloquence and professionalism

- Enhanced reputation – have audiences talk about you in increasingly positive terms

- Transformed ability to present to any audience

- Exceed your expectations – both of me and you

- Vastly reduced preparation time

- Engage audiences in a whole new way

- Get your message across every time

- Improved confidence, eloquence and presence

- Win and retain more business

- Gives you the edge – greater chance of promotion

- Differentiate and stand out from your competition

To find out more about our
Presentation Training for Groups, email us at
info@presentationskillscoaching.co.uk
or call **0208 237 5600**

THE VIP PROGRAMME
for exceptional people

This is the ultimate executive presentation and communication programme, designed for exceptional people. It is **exclusive**, limited to only ten applicants a year and designed to **differentiate you** from others, to help you stand out from your competition.

A recent survey of 1200 Chief Executives asked them essentially one question. **"What's your secret?** Why do you think you are where you are today? What one tip would you give to others?" 62% answered that the reason that they held the position they did, was because they were very good "on their feet". They were able to engage, persuade, inspire and motivate, often at very short notice.

You are probably already successful, but maybe feel that you are not as confident, fluent or engaging as fits your position. This may well be impeding your chances of reaching where you belong. You'll have observed many times that **seniority and status are no guarantee of competence or confidence.**

You'd like to be shown how to prepare a stunning and engaging presentation in **90% less time** than most people take. You want to **look, sound and be the part.** Naturally, confidently and with ease, fluency and **eloquence.**

You also want **guaranteed results and outstanding value for time.**

This could be the programme for you.

What it covers

- **Take your presenting to a whole new level of confidence, eloquence and professionalism.** Eight half day coaching sessions with Michael Trigg, one of the UK's most experienced presentation coaches. These will include rehearsal and preparation sessions for keynote speeches and presentations.

- **Personal Impact and impression.** Half a day with Sarah Setterfield, a leading image and impact consultant. Practical tools,tips and ideas on how to manage the perceptions of others.

- **Written communication.** To be able to communicate well and effectively in writing and email is a crucial executive skill. You will spend a day with Paul de Zulueta, one of the best and most experienced business writing experts in the country. This will ensure that your written communication matches the verve and impact of your presenting.

- **Dealing with the press.** When journalists want interviews - they only want to talk to the most senior executive possible. You. This is a very different skill to presenting to a captive audience. Different media have different demands. You'll spend half a day with Michael Brown, who regularly trains top figures in every field for interviews with national and international media. The coaching will be tailored to cover any possible interview with your target media.

What you can expect

- Differentiate yourself from your competition - both internal and external

- Mastery of a vital business & personal skill - the difference that makes the difference

- Greater confidence and effectiveness in dealing with the press

- Vastly enhanced perceptions from clients and colleagues

- The freedom and choice to be coached where and when you want and need

- Total focus on your unique needs and outcomes

- Complete confidentiality

- Vastly reduced preparation time

- Get your message across every time

- Enhanced reputation - have clients and colleagues talk about you in increasingly positive terms

- Transformed ability to present to any audience

- Clearer and more effective writing

- Improved confidence, eloquence and presence.

Guarantee

Your condidence and skill as a communicator will at the very least double when you work with us. Absolutely guaranteed.

If you are one of those exceptional people who want to transform the impact they make and the way they engage; save vital days of preparation and worry; and make a powerful impression on any audience , then please get in touch.

Call Michael on **0208 237 5600** or email him on michael@presentationskillscoaching.co.uk

www.presentationskillscoaching.co.uk